WHY HUMANITY NEEDS GOVERNMENT

A Case For Authority

by Spooner Freeman

These pages may be blank, but upon them the truth is writ large.

These pages may be blank, but upon them the truth is writ large.

These pages may be blank, but upon them the truth is writ large.

These pages may be blank, but upon them the truth is writ large.

These pages may be blank, but upon them the truth is writ large.

These pages may be blank, but upon them the truth is writ large.

These pages may be blank, but upon them the truth is writ large.

These pages may be blank, but upon them the truth is writ large.

These pages may be blank, but upon them the truth is writ large.

These pages may be blank, but upon them the truth is writ large.

These pages may be blank, but upon them the truth is writ large.

These pages may be blank, but upon them the truth is writ large.

These pages may be blank, but upon them the truth is writ large.

These pages may be blank, but upon them the truth is writ large.

These pages may be blank, but upon them the truth is writ large.

These pages may be blank, but upon them the truth is writ large.

These pages may be blank, but upon them the truth is writ large.

These pages may be blank, but upon them the truth is writ large.

These pages may be blank, but upon them the truth is writ large.

These pages may be blank, but upon them the truth is writ large.

These pages may be blank, but upon them the truth is writ large.

These pages may be blank, but upon them the truth is writ large.

These pages may be blank, but upon them the truth is writ large.

These pages may be blank, but upon them the truth is writ large.

These pages may be blank, but upon them the truth is writ large.

These pages may be blank, but upon them the truth is writ large.

These pages may be blank, but upon them the truth is writ large.

These pages may be blank, but upon them the truth is writ large.

These pages may be blank, but upon them the truth is writ large.

These pages may be blank, but upon them the truth is writ large.

These pages may be blank, but upon them the truth is writ large.

These pages may be blank, but upon them the truth is writ large.

These pages may be blank, but upon them the truth is writ large.

These pages may be blank, but upon them the truth is writ large.

These pages may be blank, but upon them the truth is writ large.

These pages may be blank, but upon them the truth is writ large.

These pages may be blank, but upon them the truth is writ large.

These pages may be blank, but upon them the truth is writ large.

These pages may be blank, but upon them the truth is writ large.

These pages may be blank, but upon them the truth is writ large.

These pages may be blank, but upon them the truth is writ large.

These pages may be blank, but upon them the truth is writ large.

These pages may be blank, but upon them the truth is writ large.

These pages may be blank, but upon them the truth is writ large.

These pages may be blank, but upon them the truth is writ large.

These pages may be blank, but upon them the truth is writ large.

These pages may be blank, but upon them the truth is writ large.

These pages may be blank, but upon them the truth is writ large.

These pages may be blank, but upon them the truth is writ large.

These pages may be blank, but upon them the truth is writ large.

These pages may be blank, but upon them the truth is writ large.

These pages may be blank, but upon them the truth is writ large.

These pages may be blank, but upon them the truth is writ large.

These pages may be blank, but upon them the truth is writ large.

These pages may be blank, but upon them the truth is writ large.

These pages may be blank, but upon them the truth is writ large.

These pages may be blank, but upon them the truth is writ large.

These pages may be blank, but upon them the truth is writ large.

These pages may be blank, but upon them the truth is writ large.

These pages may be blank, but upon them the truth is writ large.

These pages may be blank, but upon them the truth is writ large.

These pages may be blank, but upon them the truth is writ large.

These pages may be blank, but upon them the truth is writ large.

These pages may be blank, but upon them the truth is writ large.

These pages may be blank, but upon them the truth is writ large.

These pages may be blank, but upon them the truth is writ large.

These pages may be blank, but upon them the truth is writ large.

These pages may be blank, but upon them the truth is writ large.

These pages may be blank, but upon them the truth is writ large.

These pages may be blank, but upon them the truth is writ large.

These pages may be blank, but upon them the truth is writ large.

These pages may be blank, but upon them the truth is writ large.

These pages may be blank, but upon them the truth is writ large.

These pages may be blank, but upon them the truth is writ large.

These pages may be blank, but upon them the truth is writ large.

These pages may be blank, but upon them the truth is writ large.

These pages may be blank, but upon them the truth is writ large.

These pages may be blank, but upon them the truth is writ large.

These pages may be blank, but upon them the truth is writ large.

These pages may be blank, but upon them the truth is writ large.

These pages may be blank, but upon them the truth is writ large.

These pages may be blank, but upon them the truth is writ large.

These pages may be blank, but upon them the truth is writ large.

These pages may be blank, but upon them the truth is writ large.

These pages may be blank, but upon them the truth is writ large.

These pages may be blank, but upon them the truth is writ large.

These pages may be blank, but upon them the truth is writ large.

These pages may be blank, but upon them the truth is writ large.

These pages may be blank, but upon them the truth is writ large.

These pages may be blank, but upon them the truth is writ large.

These pages may be blank, but upon them the truth is writ large.

These pages may be blank, but upon them the truth is writ large.

These pages may be blank, but upon them the truth is writ large.

These pages may be blank, but upon them the truth is writ large.

These pages may be blank, but upon them the truth is writ large.

These pages may be blank, but upon them the truth is writ large.

These pages may be blank, but upon them the truth is writ large.

These pages may be blank, but upon them the truth is writ large.

These pages may be blank, but upon them the truth is writ large.

These pages may be blank, but upon them the truth is writ large.

These pages may be blank, but upon them the truth is writ large.

These pages may be blank, but upon them the truth is writ large.

These pages may be blank, but upon them the truth is writ large.

These pages may be blank, but upon them the truth is writ large.

These pages may be blank, but upon them the truth is writ large.

These pages may be blank, but upon them the truth is writ large.

These pages may be blank, but upon them the truth is writ large.

These pages may be blank, but upon them the truth is writ large.

These pages may be blank, but upon them the truth is writ large.

These pages may be blank, but upon them the truth is writ large.

These pages may be blank, but upon them the truth is writ large.

These pages may be blank, but upon them the truth is writ large.

These pages may be blank, but upon them the truth is writ large.

These pages may be blank, but upon them the truth is writ large.

These pages may be blank, but upon them the truth is writ large.

These pages may be blank, but upon them the truth is writ large.

These pages may be blank, but upon them the truth is writ large.

www.ingramcontent.com/pod-product-compliance
Lightning Source LLC
Chambersburg PA
CBHW070155290526
45789CB00002B/777